SIMP

BALL &

BARNES
& NOBLE
BOOKS
NEW YORK

This edition published by Barnes & Noble Inc
by arrangement with Hinkler Books Pty Ltd

2005 Barnes & Noble Books

© Hinkler Books Pty Ltd 2004
Reprinted 2005

M 10 9 8 7 6 5 4 3 2
ISBN 0 7607 72193

Art Director: Karen Moores
Editor: Rose Inserra
Design: Sam Grimmer, Katherine Power
Photography: Glenn Weiss

Printed and bound in China

CONTENTS

INTRODUCTION

Hi and welcome to *Simply Ball & Band*. This book is your guide and reference to your new fitball and resistance band workout DVD. Simply Ball & Band is presented to you by Dina Matty from *Pilates the Authentic Way* and Mark Richardson who brought you *Fighting Fit*. It is a progressive workout that has 3 classes with 3 respective levels combining a focus on strength, core stability and cardiovascular fitness.

If you have never used this equipment before, do not worry, because the class is suitable for a complete beginner who is interested in enjoying the benefits of the fitball and resistance band. Experienced fitball users are offered loads of fun and strong challenges in the advanced levels.

Simply Ball & Band keeps you
- trim with a progressive aerobic component
- toned with a gradual strength program
- happy because it enables you to have fun with the equipment provided in the comfort of your own home with the proper instruction that will see you achieving results.

Using *Simply Ball & Band* is an easy way to exercise but still includes all the major components of any professional fitness and strength program offering a beginner level through to advanced so that you can progress at your own pace. It begins with a comprehensive warm up and flexibility component and finishes with a calm, relaxing cool down.

POINTS TO REMEMBER

CORE BRACING & POSTURE

Today everyone is out to achieve maximum 'core stability'. But what is core stability and how do we strengthen our core? The core is made up of a number of different muscles located in the centre or trunk of your body and the lower back and hip. Your centre muscles include the rectus abdominus, transverse abdominus and obliques. Your lower back and hip are comprised of the gluteus medius, gluteus maximus and the adductors (inner thighs). To ensure that all strength and even cardio exercises are executed safely to prevent injury, it is important to brace and strengthen your core. This is achieved by engaging your centre muscles by drawing your tummy in and up under your ribs, or imagine your navel being pulled in toward your spine and up under your rib cage.

With certain exercises (mostly when your legs are straight) you can also engage your hip and lower back (centre muscles are also included in the lower back), by squeezing your glutes and your adductors (inner thighs). Furthermore, most exercises require a set posture in the shoulders and upper back in order to prevent injury in the upper torso. This is achieved by dropping your shoulders down and drawing your shoulder blades together. Remember, since we are all aiming for peak health and fitness, it would be unfortunate to cause an injury whilst striving to do just that, hence the importance of your core bracing and posture.

BREATHING & FOCUS

It is common for people to hold their breath during, or when executing any exercise, particularly when doing strength exercises. It is important to breathe during all your exercises, and it is most beneficial to emphasise your exhalation in time with the exertion part of the exercise to help you focus on technique and core bracing. For example, when doing push ups inhale as you lower down and exhale to push up.

CONTRAINDICATIONS

Because of the physical nature of the fitball and flexiband workout program it is advisable that you obtain permission from your family medical practitioner if you have any past or present injuries or concerns that are listed below:

- pregnancy
- high/low blood pressure
- heart disease
- joint injuries - back, neck, shoulder, elbow, wrist, hip, knee and ankle
- muscular injuries
- diabetes

Although designed for everyone, some people may be limited by personal conditions (listed above) when performing some of these exercises. For this reason and for variety, we have included variations of exercises targeting specific muscle groups.

WARM UP & STABILITY

The purpose of the warm up and stability is to stretch your body for the work out to come, familiarise yourself with the ball, and to check correct postural technique, so you can get the most benefit from your workout, whilst preventing any injuries.

BREATHING

1 Lie on your back, legs elevated on the ball, arms by your side and palms to the floor. Draw shoulder blades down and back, keeping your neck nice and long.

2 Inhale and expand your back on the mat. Exhale and draw the core muscles in and up (core muscles include transverse abdominus, obliques and rectus).

3 Inhale for three or four counts, then exhale for three or four counts.

4 Repeat twice more.

SPINAL ROTATION

1 From previous position raise arms horizontal, palms down to the floor

2 Inhale and roll the ball to one side, going as far as you can whilst keeping both shoulder blades drawn down and on the floor.

3 Exhale, draw core muscles in and to return to centre.

4 Repeat for three counts on each side

HIP STRETCH

1 From the previous position roll the ball away from you and cross the right ankle onto the left knee. Hold under the knee with both hands, reaching the left hand around the side and the right in between the legs, pressing the right knee open to feel the stretch in the hip.

2 Inhale to prepare, exhale as you stretch and press the knee away and stretch the hip.

3 Hold the stretch for three or four counts.

4 Repeat on other side.

CORE FLEXION

1 Place both feet on the ball, draw the ball into the back of your legs and place your fingertips lightly on the back of your head (don't pull on your neck).

2 Inhale, curl up and forward, hold for two counts then release back down.

3 Inhale to prepare and exhale as you hold, drawing the core muscles in and up.

4 Repeat four more times.

SPINAL MASSAGE

1 From previous position, pick the ball up with your feet and pass the ball to your hands. Keep your legs in table-top position (knees over your hips, shins horizontal).

2 Draw your core muscles in and up.

3 Draw your chin to your chest, gently rocking forward and back three to five times, massaging the spine.

4 On your final rock forward sit up, crossing your legs.

WARM UP & STABILITY

(continued)

LOWER BACK & HIP STRETCH

1 From the previous position (legs crossed), roll the ball forward walking your hands down the ball, draw your chin to your chest.

2 Inhale, extending from the lower back. Exhale while gently folding forward.

3 Hold for three or four counts.

4 Roll the ball slowly back to the original position.

HAMSTRING & INNER THIGH STRETCH

1 Extend both legs to the side, poir knees and toes to the ceiling.

2 Walk the ball forward gently, stretching the hamstring and add (inner thigh) muscles.

3 Inhale, drawing your core muscle and up, exhale and stretch.

4 Hold the stretch for three to four counts and walk the ball back to original position.

5 Repeat Lower Back & Hip Stretch on the other side.

BACK STRETCH

1 Come up onto your knees, sit your hips back onto your heels, walk the ball forward so that your back is flat and you feel the stretch in your back and sides of your torso.

2 Draw your core muscles in and up as you move forward.

3 Inhale to prepare and exhale as you walk the ball forward into the stretch.

4 Hold the stretch for three to four counts.

HORIZONTAL SIDE STRETCH

1 From the previous position, keep the hips back on the heels, roll the ball to one side, walking the hands over the ball so you can feel the stretch in the lats (the muscle by your ribs).

2 Inhale as you walk over and exhale as you stretch.

3 Draw your core muscles in and up as you hold the stretch for three to four counts.

4 Repeat on the other side.

CAT CURL STRETCH

1 Walk the ball back to the centre, raise your hips off your heels, walk out to a flat back position.

2 Inhale to prepare, exhale pulling up into the cat curl stretch.

3 Draw your core muscles in and up to feel the stretch across the middle of your back.

4 Hold the stretch three to four counts.

PRONE STABILITY

1 Walk the ball back in, lay your stomach over the ball and place your hands in front of you. Roll forward on the ball, extend the legs and keep your toes on the floor, keeping your shoulders down and back.

2 Return to the start position, walk forward to the hips. This time raise legs in the air and draw core muscles in and up.

3 Return to the start position, walk forward to the thigh and hold for three to four counts.

4 Repeat step 3.

WARM UP & STABILITY

(continued)

HIP FLEXOR, CALF & ACHILLES STRETCH

1 Roll the ball to one side, place your hand on the ball and step the opposite leg forward with your knee in line with your ankle. Keep your back knee on the floor to stretch your hip flexor.

2 Draw your core muscles in and up to stay out of your back.

3 Hold for three to four counts.

4 Lift your back knee off the floor, sinking your hips low to the floor to increase the stretch. Hold for three to four counts.

5 Lift your weight, draw the back foot forward and place your heel down. Keep your weight forward and stretch your calf and achilles. Hold for three to four counts.

6 Bring feet together, roll the ball to the other side and repeat Hip Flexor, Calf & Achilles Stretch on the other side.

CORE ROTATION

1 Stand up, feet hip width apart and ball at hip height. With your ball turn to one side transferring your weight onto that foot, twisting your core and looking over your shoulder. Repeat on the other side, then repeat this at chest then shoulder heights and return back down to the hips.

2 Draw core muscles in and up, keeping your hips square to the front. Rotate from the waist during the whole exercise.

3 Place the ball on the floor, walk around to the front and sit on the ball.

Warm Up & Stability

(continued)

Imprinting & Leg Extension

1 Sit tall on your ball, drawing your core muscles in and up, with your shoulders back and hands by your side. Maintain this posture and lift one heel off the floor. Hold for one count and repeat on the other side.

2 Maintain the above position and lift your whole foot off the floor, staying tall and keeping balance. Hold for one count then repeat on the other side.

3 Keep the previous posture, raise your foot off the floor and flex your leg upward at the knee, staying tall and keeping balance. Hold for two counts and repeat on the other side.

Bridging

1 Maintaining the above position, dr your core muscles in and up, and walk forward so your lower back is on the ball. Hold for two counts, then wa back to the original position, keeping your shoulders forward over your hips

2 Repeat again so that your shoulde blades reach the ball. Hold for two counts and return to the original position.

3 Repeat again so that your head an shoulders are on the ball in full bridge position, keep your hips lifted b squeezing your glutes. Hold for three t four counts and return to the original position.

4 Repeat step three.

SINGLE HAMSTRING STRETCH

1 Sit tall on your ball, extending one leg forward with your heel on the floor and your toes pointing to the ceiling.

2 Inhale, drawing your core muscles in and up. Exhale and lean forward, maintaining a long spine. Stretch the hamstring.

3 Hold the stretch for three to four counts.

4 Repeat on the other leg.

DOUBLE HAMSTRING STRETCH

1 Sit tall on your ball.

2 Draw your core muscles in and up, extend your knees, rolling the ball back. Lean forward, sliding your hands down your legs.

3 Inhale to prepare, and exhale using your hands to pull yourself gently toward your legs.

4 Hold for three to four counts.

5 Draw your core muscles in and up as you roll your spine back to the original position.

WARM UP & STABILITY

(continued)

SIDE STRETCH

1 Sit tall on your ball with your feet wide and place one elbow on your thigh.

2 Draw your core muscles in and up.

3 Inhale and lift your opposite arm up to your ear. While exhaling, increase the stretch over to the side.

4 Hold for three to four counts.

SIDE & LAT STRETCH

1 From the last position, twist forward, reaching your opposite arm, palm to the front.

2 Hold for three to four counts.

NECK STRETCH

1 From the last position, draw your core muscles in and up to pull yourself into a seated position. Sit tall.

2 Inhale as you place your resting hand behind your back and your opposite hand over your head. Exhale and gently pull your ear to your shoulder, stretching your neck.

3 Hold for three to four counts.

4 Repeat the Side Stretch, Side & Lat Stretch, and then the Neck Stretch on the other side.

Level 1 Workout

Cardio Set A

Strength Set A (Chest)
Thigh Push Up
Bridging Chest Press

Cardio Set B

Strength Set B (Back & Biceps)
Prone Back Extension
Seated Row

Cardio Set C

Strength Set C (Legs)
Squat
Wall Squat

Cardio Set D

Strength Set D (Abdominals)
Assisted Single Leg Lower & Lift
Assisted Core Flexion

Cardio Set E

Strength Set E (Triceps)
Overhead Tricep Extension with Band
Overhead Tricep Extension with Ball

INTRODUCTION TO LEVEL 1 WORKOUT

CARDIO

The exercises in this level are performed predominantly seated on the ball, offering a low impact cardiovascular workout. It is important to be aware of your posture, pulling your core muscles in and up for good alignment and balance. Your aim is to be confidently centred on the ball for all the exercises at this level whilst aiming to keep the same speed as your instructors on the DVD. Once you have achieved this, move on to level 2 cardio.

STRENGTH

The exercises in this level develop a strong foundation in your basic core strength. The emphasis at this level is to be aware of your core muscles, drawing them inward and upward, and drawing your shoulders down and back. Squeeze your glutes and inner thighs when appropriate. Additionally, you should be aiming to complete eight to ten reps of all the exercises, with a 1-2-1 tempo. The tempo applies to the length of time of (1) the initial movement, (2) the holding position and (3) the return to the original position, respectively. When you have reached this goal with strong core strength, good technique and the correct tempo, challenge yourself further and move onto the next level.

LEVEL 1 CARDIO SET A

BOUNCING	X 8
SIDE TAP	X 8
BOUNCING	X 8
SIDE TAP	X 8
STAR JUMP	X 8
BOUNCING	X 8
SIDE TAP	X 8
STAR JUMP	X 8

Bouncing

Side Tap

Star Jump

LEVEL 1 STRENGTH SET A - CHEST

THIGH PUSH UP

1 Squat behind the ball, roll forward so your thighs are over the ball, shoulders over and in line with the wrists, palms on the floor.

2 Draw your core muscles in and up with shoulders down and back. Squeeze your glutes and inner thighs.

3 Inhale, bend your elbows to the side and lower your chest to the floor. Exhale and push up. Return to the original position.

4 Lower for one count, hold the position for two counts and push up for one count.

BRIDGING CHEST PRESS

1 Sitting tall on your ball, walk out to the full bridge position, place your hands up and together above your shoulders.

2 Keeping your neck long and your shoulders down, draw your core muscles in and up and squeeze your glutes and inner thighs to keep your hips raised.

3 Picture a triangle where your hands are at the top point, inhaling as you lower your hands to the lower points of the triangle. Exhale and push your hands to the top.

4 With your own resistance or tension, lower yourself down for one count, hold for two counts, and push back up for one count.

Level 1 Cardio Set B

Bouncing	x 8
Side Tap	x 8
Star Jump	x 8
Bouncing add Reach & Pull	x 8
Side Tap add Jab	x 8
Star Jump add Shoulder Press	x 8
Bouncing with Reach & Pull	x 8
Side Tap with Jab	x 8
Star Jump with Shoulder Press	x 8

Bouncing

Side Tap

Star Jump

Bouncing add Reach & Pull

Side Tap add Jab

Star Jump add Shoulder Press

LEVEL 1 STRENGTH SET B– BACK & BICEPS

PRONE BACK EXTENSION

1 Squat behind the ball and roll forward. Your hips should be on the ball with your legs extended and your toes tucked under and touching the floor. Place your fingertips on the back of your head and fold forward.

2 Squeeze your glutes and pull in and up with your core muscles.

3 Inhale to prepare, exhale as you extend at the hip, raising your upper body to a prone position above the floor.

4 Lift for one count, hold for two counts and lower in one count.

SEATED ROW

1 Sitting tall on the ball, place both feet over the middle of your band. Wrap the ends around your hands, reaching your arms' length.

2 Draw the core muscles in and up.

3 Inhale to prepare, exhale and pull the band, drawing your elbows just past your ribs. Squeeze your shoulder blade to open up your chest.

4 Pull back for one count, hold for two counts and release for one count.

LEVEL 1 CARDIO SET C

Bouncing with Reach & Pull	X 8
Side Tap with Jab	X 8
Star Jump with Shoulder Press	X 8
Squat & Lift	X 4
Squat & Lift (Double Time)	X 8
Squat & Lift	X 4
Squat & Lift (Double Time)	X 8

Bouncing with Reach & Pull

Star Jump with Shoulder Press

Side Tap with Jab

Squat & Lift

LEVEL 1 STRENGTH SET C - LEGS

SQUAT

1 Stand with your feet parallel and hip width apart, sit your hips back so your weight is over your heels.

2 As you inhale, squat down aiming to lower your hips level with your knees so you can just see your toes over your knees. Hold while drawing the core muscles in and up.

3 Exhale as you push up from your heels, squeezing your glutes to a standing position.

4 Lower for one count. Hold the squat for two counts and push up for one count.

WALL SQUAT

1 Place the ball on the wall and lean the curve of your back against the ball. Position your feet parallel and hip width apart, and sit your hips back so that your weight is over your heels.

2 Inhale to lower, supporting your lower back at all times with the ball, aiming to keep your hips in line with your knees so you can just see your toes over your knees.

3 Exhale as you push up from your heels, squeezing your glutes to a standing position.

4 Lower for one count. Hold the squat for two counts and push up for one count.

LEVEL 1 CARDIO SET D

BOUNCING WITH REACH & PULL	X 8
SIDE TAP WITH JAB	X 8
STAR JUMP WITH SHOULDER PRESS	X 8
SQUAT & LIFT (DOUBLE TIME)	X 8
(WALK AROUND BALL TO) SQUAT TAP	X 3
(WALK BALL THROUGH LEGS AND SIT)	
SQUAT & LIFT (DOUBLE TIME)	X 8
(WALK AROUND BALL TO) SQUAT TAP	X 3
(WALK BALL THROUGH LEGS AND SIT)	

Bouncing with Reach & Pull

Side Tap with Jab

Star Jump with Shoulder Press

Squat & Lift

Squat & Tap

Level 1 Strength Set D - Abdominals

Assisted Single Leg Lower Lift

1 Lie on the floor with your legs over the ball so that your calves and thighs are in contact with the ball. Place your arms by your sides, palms down.

2 Draw your core muscles in and up so your lower back is on the floor.

3 Inhale as you lower your heel to the floor keeping your knee bent, and exhale as you draw your core muscles in raising your leg back to the ball.

4 Lower your leg for one count, hold for two counts and lift for one count.

Assisted Core Flexion

1 Lie on the band so your band is aligned with your spine. Place your legs over the ball making sure that calves and thighs are in contact with the ball.

2 Hold your band at the outside edges, pulling on the band to create a nice strong tension. Keep your elbow open so as not to pull on your neck.

3 Inhale to prepare, curl your head and shoulders forward. Exhale and draw your core muscles in and up, then release down to the floor.

4 Lift for one count, hold for two counts and release to the floor in one.

Level 1 Cardio Set E

Bouncing with Reach & Pull	x 8
Side Tap with Jab	x 8
Star Jump with Shoulder Press	x 8
Squat & Lift (Double Time)	x 8
(Walk around ball to) Squat Tap	x 3
(Walk ball through legs and sit)	
Squat & Lift (Double Time)	x 8
(Walk around ball to) Squat Tap	x 3
(Walk ball through legs and sit)	

Bouncing with Reach & Pull

Side Tap with Jab

Walk Ball through Legs & Sit

Star Jump with Shoulder Press   Squat & Lift   Squat & Tap

Level 1 Strength Set E-Triceps

Overhead Tricep Extension with Band

1 Sit tall on the band on your ball. With feet hip width apart, hold your band at the outside edges and pull on the band. This will create a nice strong tension.

2 Pull your core muscles in and up, keeping your elbows close to your head.

3 Inhale to prepare, and exhale as you raise your hands above your head, extending your elbows. Flex your triceps.

4 Raise for one count, hold the extension for two counts, and release for one count.

Overhead Tricep Extension with Ball

1 Stand in a comfortable position and hold your ball with your arms extended over your head.

2 Keep your weight forward onto the balls of your feet, drawing your core muscles in and up.

3 Inhale to lower the ball down to the back of your head, keeping your elbow close to your head. Exhale while raising the ball and extending at the elbows. Flex your triceps.

4 Lower in one count, hold for two counts, and extend for one count.

Level 2 Workout

Cardio Set A

Strength Set A (Chest)
Bridging Chest Press with Band
Shin Push Up

Cardio Set B

Strength Set B (Back & Biceps)
Seated Row with Leg Extension
Prone Back Extension with Lat Pulldown

Cardio Set C

Strength Set C (Legs)
Wall Lunge
Lunge with Shoulder Press

Cardio Set D

Strength Set D (Abdominals)
Ball in Hands Core Flexion
Double Leg Lower & Lift

Cardio Set E

Strength Set E (Triceps)
Prone Tricep Extension
Prone Tricep Extension with Band

INTRODUCTION TO LEVEL 2 WORKOUT

CARDIO

The exercises in this level are performed standing up, using the ball to increase the intensity. This low impact cardiovascular workout utilises dynamic footwork, longer levers and a more complex choreography. It is important to be aware of your posture, pulling your core muscles in and up for good alignment and balance. Your aim is to be able to confidently perform all the exercises at this level whilst aiming to keep the same speed as your instructors on the DVD. For an extra challenge try performing all the level 2 cardio blocks in a row, just by queuing forward on your DVD. Then try level 3 cardio.

STRENGTH

Level 2 strength still focuses on core strength whilst progressing the exercises to an intermediate level with more balance and stability control, therefore promoting increased strength. At this level you should be aiming to complete eight to ten reps of all the exercises, with a 1-3-1 tempo. When you have reached this goal with strong core strength, good technique and the correct tempo, challenge yourself further and move onto the next level.

Level 2 Cardio Set A

WALK FORWARD TAP	X 2
WALK FORWARD KNEE	X 2
SIDE TAP	X 8
WALK FORWARD KNEE ADD SHOULDER PRESS	X 2
SIDE TAP ADD CHEST PRESS	X 8
WALK FORWARD KNEE WITH SHOULDER PRESS	X 2
SIDE TAP WITH CHEST PRESS	X 8

Walk Forward Tap

Walk Forward Knee

Walk Forward Knee add Shoulder Press

Side Tap with Chest Press

Side Tap

LEVEL 2 STRENGTH SET A-CHEST

BRIDGING CHEST PRESS WITH BAND

1 Sitting tall on your ball, place the band on the floor in front of the ball. Hold each end of the band and walk out to the full bridge position so that the ball is over the band. Place your hands up and together above your shoulders.

2 Keeping your neck long and your shoulders down, draw your core muscles in and up and squeeze your glutes and inner thighs to keep your hips raised.

3 Picture a triangle where your hands are at the top point. Inhale as you lower your hands to the lower points of the triangle and exhale while pushing your hands to the top using the resistance of the band.

4 Lowering down for one count, hold for three counts. Then push back up for one count.

SHIN PUSH UP

1 Squat behind the ball and roll forward so that your shins are over the ball, your shoulders over and in line with the wrists, palms on the floor.

2 Draw your core muscles in and up with shoulders down and back and squeeze your glutes and inner thighs.

3 Inhale, bend your elbows to the side and lower your chest to the floor. Exhale, push up and return to the original position.

4 Lower for one count, hold the position for three counts and push up for one count.

LEVEL 2 CARDIO SET B

WALK FORWARD KNEE WITH SHOULDER PRESS	X 2
SIDE TAP WITH CHEST PRESS	X 8
STEP TOUCH	X 8
DOUBLE STEP TOUCH	X 4
STEP TOUCH ADD BOUNCE	X 8
DOUBLE STEP TOUCH ADD FULL CIRCLE	X 4
STEP TOUCH WITH BOUNCE	X 8
DOUBLE STEP TOUCH WITH FULL CIRCLE	X 4

Walk Forward Knee with Shoulder Press

Side Tap with Chest Press

Step Touch with Bounce

Double Step Touch with Full Circle

LEVEL 2 STRENGTH SET B – BACK & BICEPS

SEATED ROW WITH LEG EXTENSION

1 Sitting tall on the ball, placing both feet over the middle of your band, wrap the ends around your hands. Lift one foot up and extend leg at the knee joint for the leg extension.

2 Draw the core muscles in and up.

3 Inhale to prepare, exhale and pull using the resistance of the band, drawing your elbows just past your ribs. Squeeze your shoulder blade to open up your chest. Aim for five repetitions, then repeat on the opposite leg.

4 Pull back for one count, hold for three counts and release for one count.

PRONE BACK EXTENSION WITH LAT PULLDOWN

1 Squat behind the ball and roll forward. Your hips should be on the ball with your legs extended and your toes tucked under and touching the floor. Place your fingertips on the back of your head and fold forward.

2 Squeeze your glutes and pull in and up with your core muscles.

3 Inhale to prepare, exhale as you extend at the hip, raising your upper body to a prone position over the floor. Inhale and reach your arms forward, then exhale and draw your elbows into the ribs, squeezing your lats and upper back. Inhale and place your fingertips behind your head and exhale as you lower yourself down.

4 Lift for one count, extend and flex the arms for three counts, and lower in one count.

LEVEL 2 CARDIO SET C

WALK FORWARD KNEE WITH SHOULDER PRESS	X 2
SIDE TAP WITH CHEST PRESS	X 8
STEP TOUCH WITH BOUNCE	X 8
DOUBLE STEP TOUCH WITH FULL CIRCLE	X 4
STEP TOUCH WITH BOUNCE	X 8
DOUBLE STEP TOUCH WITH FULL CIRCLE ADD SKIP	X 4
STEP TOUCH WITH BOUNCE	X 8
DOUBLE STEP TOUCH WITH FULL CIRCLE WITH SKIP	X 4

Side Tap with Chest Press

Walk Forward Knee with Shoulder Press   Step Touch with Bounce   Double Step Touch with Full C

LEVEL 2 STRENGTH SET C-LEGS

WALL LUNGE

1 Place the ball on the wall and lean the curve of your back against the ball. Position your feet one foot forward and one foot back with hip width apart. Make sure that your weight is centred over your front heel.

2 Inhale as you lower your body, supporting your lower back at all times with the ball. Aim to keep your hips in line with your knee so you can just see your toes over your knee.

3 Exhale while pushing up from your heel to standing position.

4 Lower for one count, hold the lunge for three counts, and push up for one count then repeat on the other leg.

LUNGE WITH SHOULDER PRESS

1 Stand with your feet parallel and hip width apart. Sit your hips in a backward position so that your weight is over your heels, holding your ball at chest level.

2 As you inhale, squat down aiming to lower your hips level with your knees so that you can just see your toes over your knees. Hold, drawing the core muscles in and up and reach the ball over your head.

3 Exhale while pushing up from your heels, squeezing your glutes to a standing position and lowering the ball to the chest.

4 Lower for one count, hold the squat for three counts, and push up for one count then repeat on the other leg.

LEVEL 2 CARDIO SET D

WALK FORWARD KNEE WITH SHOULDER PRESS	X 2
SIDE TAP WITH CHEST PRESS	X 8
STEP TOUCH WITH BOUNCE	X 8
DOUBLE STEP TOUCH WITH FULL CIRCLE & SKIP	X 4
SQUAT & LIFT	X 4
SQUAT & KNEE	X 4

Side Tap with Chest Press

Walk Forward Knee with Shoulder Press

Step Touch with Bounce

Double Step Touch with Full Circle & Skip

Squat and Knee

Level 2 Strength Set D - Abdominals

Ball in Hands Core Flexion

1 Lie on your back, ball in hands reaching to the ceiling and legs in table-top position.

2 Inhale while curling up and forward, reaching the ball towards your shins.

3 Exhale and hold, drawing core muscles in and up and release. Make sure that your back does not arch off the floor.

4 Lift for one count, hold for three counts and release to the floor in one.

Double Leg Lower Lift

1 Lie on the floor, ball in hands reaching to the ceiling and legs in table-top position.

2 Draw your core muscles in and up so that your lower back is not arching off the floor.

3 Inhale as you lower your heel(s) to the floor keeping your knee(s) bent. Exhale as you draw your core muscles in, raising your leg back to the table-top position. Repeat, alternating legs for four reps then add the double leg for two reps for a harder variation.

4 Lower your leg(s) for one count, hold for three counts and lift for one count.

LEVEL 2 CARDIO SET E

WALK FORWARD KNEE WITH SHOULDER PRESS	X 2
SIDE TAP WITH CHEST PRESS	X 8
STEP TOUCH WITH BOUNCE	X 8
DOUBLE STEP TOUCH WITH FULL CIRCLE & SKIP	X 4
SQUAT & KNEE	X 4

Side Tap with Chest Press

Walk Forward Knee with Shoulder Press

Step Touch with Bounce

Double Step Touch with Full Circle and Skip

Squat and Knee

LEVEL 2 STRENGTH SET E - TRICEPS

PRONE TRICEP EXTENSION

1 Squat behind the ball and roll forward. Your hips should be on the ball with your legs extended and your toes tucked under and touching the floor. Pull your elbows just past your ribs, holding your fists at chest height.

2 Pull your core muscles in and up, keeping your elbows close to the sides of your body. Extend your elbows, reaching your arms back, so that your hands are above hip level.

3 Inhale to prepare, and exhale as you extend your elbows.

4 Extend for one count, hold the extension for three counts, and release for one count.

PRONE TRICEP EXTENSION WITH BAND

1 Squat behind the ball, placing the band in front of the ball on the floor. Roll forward and hold the ends of the band. Your hips should be on the ball with your legs extended and your toes tucked under and touching the floor. Pull your elbows just past your ribs, holding your fists at chest height.

2 Pull your core muscles in and up, keeping your elbows close to the sides of your body. Extend your elbows using the resistance of the band, reaching your arms back, so that your hands are above hip level.

3 Inhale to prepare, and exhale as you extend your elbows.

4 Extend for one count, hold the extension for three counts, and release for one count.

LEVEL 3 WORKOUT

CARDIO SET A

STRENGTH SET A (CHEST)
Hands on the Ball Push Up
Single Leg Push Up

CARDIO SET B

STRENGTH SET B (BACK & BICEPS)
Bent Over Row with Band
Prone Back Extension with Twist (Mega)

CARDIO SET C

STRENGTH SET C (LEGS)
Lunge on the Ball
Squat Hold with Shoulder Press

CARDIO SET D

STRENGTH SET D (ABDOMINALS)
Core Flexion with Double Leg Lower & Lift
Overhead Reach with Double Leg Stretch

CARDIO SET E

STRENGTH SET E (TRICEPS)
Wall Dips
Unassisted Dips

INTRODUCTION TO LEVEL 3 WORKOUT

CARDIO

Level 3 cardio is a progressive workout that starts to build upon itself. Exercises from both previous levels have been utilised, creating an intricate workout using seated and standing movements that you will already have confidence in doing. This level will challenge you physically and mentally, integrating dynamic footwork, longer levers and complex choreography. It is important to be aware of your posture, pulling your core muscles in and up for good alignment and balance. Your aim is to be able to confidently perform all the exercises at this level whilst aiming to keep the same speed as your instructors on the DVD. For an extra challenge try performing all the level 3 cardio blocks in a row, just by queuing forward on your DVD.

STRENGTH

At this stage you will have a strong foundation in your core strength. This will allow you to progress to where you will be challenged technically at many levels. These exercises involve emphasis in posture, balance, control, strength and endurance. You should be aiming to complete eight to ten reps of all the exercises, with a 2-3-2 tempo, strong core strength and good technique. If you are confident in performing level 3 strength in this format, try performing all the strength together without the interruption of the cardio workouts, by queuing your DVD forward.

Level 3 Cardio Set A

Bouncing with Reach & Pull	x 8
Side Tap with Jab	x 8
Star Jump with Shoulder Press	x 8
Squat & Lift (Double Time)	x 8
(Walk around ball to) Squat Tap	x 3
(Walk ball through legs and sit)	
Squat & Lift (Double Time)	x 8
(Walk around ball to) Squat Tap	x 3
(Walk ball through legs and sit)	

Bouncing with Reach & Pull

Side Tap with Jab

Walk Ball through Legs & Sit

Star Jump with Shoulder Press

Squat & Lift

Squat & Tap

LEVEL 3 STRENGTH SET A-CHEST

HANDS ON BALL PUSH UP

1 Place your hands on the ball and walk your feet back into the push up position.

2 Draw your core muscles in and up with shoulders down and back. Squeeze your glutes and inner thighs.

3 Inhale, bend your elbows to the side and lower your chest to the ball. Exhale as you push up and return to the original position.

4 Lower for two counts, hold the position for three counts and push up for two counts.

SINGLE LEG PUSH UP

1 Squat behind the ball, rolling forward so that your shins are over the ball, shoulders over and in line with the wrists, palms on the floor.

2 Draw your core muscles in and up, shoulders down and back. Squeeze your glutes and inner thighs, raising one leg off the ball.

3 Inhale, bend your elbows to the side and lower your chest to the floor. Exhale and push up. Return to the original position.

4 Lower for two counts, hold the position for three counts and push up for two counts.

Level 3 Cardio Set B

Walk Forward Knee with Shoulder Press	x 2
Side Tap with Chest Press	x 8
Step Touch with Bounce	x 8
Double Step Touch with Full Circle & Skip	x 4
Squat & Knee	x 4

Walk Forward Knee with Shoulder Press

Side Tap with Chest Press

Step Touch with Bounce

Double Step Touch with Full Circle and Skip

Squat and Knee

LEVEL 3 STRENGTH SET B - BACK & BICEPS

BENT OVER ROW WITH BAND

1 Stand behind the ball, placing one foot over the middle of the band. Wrap the ends of the band around your opposite hand and place the other on the ball.

2 Lean forward, drawing your core muscles in and up in flat back position, with one foot forward and the other foot back.

3 Inhale to prepare, exhale to pull your elbow up just past the ribs, and hand to the chest level, using the resistance of the band.

4 Pull for two counts, hold for three, and release for two counts.

PRONE BACK EXTENSION WITH TWIST (MEGA)

1 Squat behind the ball and roll forward. Your hips should be on the ball with your legs extended and your toes tucked under and touching the floor. Place your fingertips on the back of your head and fold forward.

2 Squeeze your glutes and pull in and up with your core muscles.

3 Inhale to prepare, exhale as you extend at the hip, raising your upper body to a prone position over the floor. Inhale and reach your arms forward. Exhale and draw your elbows into the ribs, squeezing your lats and upper back. Inhale and place your fingertips behind your head and exhale, twisting at the waist and aiming your elbow to the ceiling. Keep your chest and shoulders open at all times.

4 Lift for two count, extend and flex the arms and twist for three, and lower in two counts.

Level 3 Cardio Set C

Bouncing with Reach & Pull	X 8
Side Tap with Jab	X 8
Star Jump with Shoulder Press	X 8
Squat & Lift (Double Time)	X 8
(Walk around ball to) Squat Tap	X 3
(Walk ball through legs and sit)	
Squat & Lift (Double Time)	X 8
(Walk around ball to) Squat Tap	X 3
(Walk ball through legs and sit)	

Bouncing with Reach & Pull

Side Tap with Jab

Star Jump with Shoulder Press

Squat & Lift

Squat & Tap

Walk Ball through Legs & Sit

LEVEL 3 STRENGTH SET C - LEGS

LUNGE ON THE BALL

1 With the ball behind you, place your foot on the ball. Keeping balance, roll the ball further behind you so that your front foot is three foot lengths in front of the ball. Ensure that your weight is centred over your front heel.

2 Inhale to lower, aiming to keep your hips in line with your knee so that you can just see your toes over your knee. Simultaneously raise your hands horizontally to the front.

3 Exhale, drawing your core muscles in and up and push up from your heel to the standing position, lowering your hands.

4 Lower for two counts, hold the lunge for three, and push up for two counts then repeat on the other leg.

SQUAT HOLD WITH SHOULDER PRESS

1 Stand with your feet parallel and hip width apart and sit your hips back so that your weight is over your heels. Hold the ball at chest level.

2 As you inhale, squat down aiming to lower your hips level with your knees so that you can just see your toes over your

knees. Hold, drawing the core muscles in and up and press the ball above your head.

3 Exhale, as you push up from your heels, squeezing your glutes to the standing position.

4 Lower for two counts, hold the squat for three, and push up for two counts.

Level 3 Cardio Set D

Walk Forward Knee with Shoulder Press	x 2
Side Tap with Chest Press	x 8
Step Touch with Bounce	x 8
Double Step Touch with Full Circle & Skip	x 4
Squat & Knee	x 4

Walk Forward Knee with Shoulder Press

Side Tap with Chest Press

Step Touch with Bounce

Double Step Touch with Full Circle and Skip

Squat and Knee

LEVEL 3 STRENGTH SET D - ABDOMINALS

CORE FLEXION WITH DOUBLE LEG LOWER & LIFT

1 Lie on your back on the floor, ball in hands reaching to the ceiling with legs in table-top position.

2 Draw your chin to your chest, curling up and forward. Make sure that you draw your core muscles in and up so that your lower back is not arching off the floor.

3 Inhale as you lower your heels to the floor keeping your knees bent, and exhale as you draw your core muscles in, raising your legs back to table-top position.

4 Lower your legs for two counts, hold for three and lift for two counts.

OVERHEAD REACH WITH DOUBLE LEG STRETCH

1 Lie on your back on the floor, in core flexion position with the ball over your shins.

2 Draw your core muscles in and up so that your back remains flat and is not arching.

3 Inhale as you reach your arms to your ears, stretching your legs forward at a 45-degree angle. Exhale, using your core muscles to draw back to the starting position.

4 Stretch out for two counts, hold for three, and draw in for two counts.

Level 3 Cardio Set E

Bouncing with Reach & Pull	x 8
Side Tap with Jab	x 8
Star Jump with Shoulder Press	x 8
Squat & Lift (Double Time)	x 8
(Walk around ball to) Squat Tap	x 3
(Walk ball through legs and sit)	
Squat & Lift (Double Time)	x 8
(Walk around ball to) Squat Tap	x 3
(Pick up the ball)	
Walk Forward Knee with Shoulder Press	x 2
Side Tap with Chest Press	x 8
Step Touch with Bounce	x 8
Double Step Touch with Full Circle & Skip	x 4
Squat & Knee	x 4

LEVEL 3 STRENGTH SET E-TRICEPS

WALL DIPS

1 Place the ball on the floor against the wall, sit tall on the ball and place your hands close to your hips. Walk the feet forward and slide your hips off the ball.

2 Draw your core muscles in and up and pull up out of your shoulders and wrists.

3 Inhale, bending at your elbows so that your shoulders are at elbow level. Do not roll your shoulders forward. Exhale as you push up to the starting position.

4 Lower for two counts, hold the dip for three, and push up for two counts.

UNASSISTED DIPS

1 Place the ball on the floor, sit tall on the ball and place your hands close to your hips. Walk the feet forward and slide your hips off the ball.

2 For good balance, emphasise your core stability as you draw your core muscles in and up and pull up out of your shoulders and wrists.

3 Inhale, bending at your elbows so that your shoulders are at elbow level. Do not roll your shoulders forward. Exhale as you push up to the starting position.

4 Lower for two counts, hold the dip for three, and push up for two counts.

COOL DOWN & STRETCH

The purpose of the cool down is to take the opportunity to stretch, increasing your flexibility and range of movement whilst your body is warm. Your increased flexibility will enable an improved performance of your cardiovascular and strength exercises in future workouts. Take this time to relax and wind down after you have worked at a high intensity.

BREATHING

1 Lie on your back, legs elevated on the ball, arms by your side and palms to the floor. Draw shoulder blades down the back and keep your neck nice and long.

2 Inhale and expand your back on the mat. Exhale and draw the core muscles in and up (core muscles include transverse abdominus, obliques, rectus).

3 Inhale for three or four counts, then exhale for three or four counts.

4 Repeat twice more.

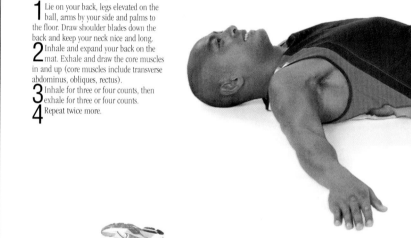

Spinal Rotation

1 From the previous position raise your arms in a horizontal position, palms down to the floor.

2 Inhale and roll the ball to one side. Go as far as you can whilst keeping both shoulder blades drawn down and on the floor.

3 Exhale, drawing core muscles in and up to return to centre.

4 Repeat three times on each side.

Hip & Hamstring Stretch

1 From the previous position roll the ball away from you and cross the right ankle onto the left knee. Hold under the knee with both hands, reaching the left hand around the side and the right in between the legs, pressing the right knee open to feel the stretch in the hip.

2 Inhale to prepare, exhale as you stretch and press the knee away and stretch the hip.

3 Hold the stretch for three or four counts.

4 Extend the leg at the knee and point to the ceiling, placing your hands around your thigh, calf or ankle, depending on your flexibility.

5 Inhale to prepare, then exhale, drawing your leg towards your body allowing you to stretch your hamstring.

6 Hold the stretch for three to four counts.

7 Repeat on the other side.

COOL DOWN & STRETCH

(continued)

SPINAL MASSAGE

1 From the previous position, pick the ball up with your feet and pass the ball to your hands, keeping your legs in the table-top position (knees over your hips, shins horizontal).

2 Draw your core muscles in and up.

3 Draw your chin to your chest, gently rocking forward and back three to five times, massaging the spine.

4 On your final rock forward, sit up and cross your legs.

LOWER BACK & HIP STRETCH

1 From the previous position (legs crossed), roll the ball forward walking your hands down the ball. Draw your chin to your chest.

2 Inhale, extending from the lower back, exhale gently folding forward.

3 Hold for three or four counts.

4 Roll the ball slowly back to the original position.

HAMSTRING & INNER THIGH STRETCH

1 Extend both legs to the side, pointing knees and toes to the ceiling.

2 Walk the ball forward gently, stretching the hamstring and adductor (inner thigh) muscles.

3 Inhale, draw in your core muscles in and up, exhale and stretch.

4 Hold the stretch for three to four counts and walk the ball back to the original position.

5 Repeat Lower Back & Hip Stretch on the other side.

Cool Down & Stretch

(continued)

Side Stretch

1 Sit on the floor with the ball to one side, in crossed legs position and place one arm on the ball.

2 Draw your core muscles in and up.

3 Inhale, lift your opposite arm up to your ear. While exhaling, increase the stretch over to the side.

4 Hold for three to four counts.

Neck Stretch

1 From the last position, draw your core muscles in and up to pull yourself into a seated position. Sit tall.

2 Inhale, placing your opposite hand over your head, and exhale, gently pulling your ear to your shoulder and stretching your neck.

3 Hold for three to four counts.

CHEST &
SHOULDER
STRETCH

1 Sitting tall in a crossed leg position, place the ball behind you. Aim to place both hands on either side of the ball.

2 Inhale, drawing you core muscles in and up.

3 Exhaling, squeeze your upper back together which will open your chest and shoulder.

4 Hold the stretch for three to four counts.

5 Bring the ball to the other side and repeat the Side Stretch and Neck Stretch on the other side.

CONCLUSION

Simply Ball & Band gives you the flexibility to train any time at home. Remember that practice makes perfect. To achieve maximum results and to realise the full benefits, it is advisable to be able to confidently perform each level before moving on to the next level. Optimal cardiovascular fitness and strength and endurance at each level will be realised when you can perform all the cardio blocks together, followed by all the strength training exercises, each without rest. You will then be well on your way to the next level. For the ultimate experience, join the cardiovascular workouts from level 1, 2, and 3, and likewise with the strength exercises. Perform all these without a rest.

At beginner level it is advisable to train twice a week. For those who would like to achieve their goals faster or who are advanced, training three to four times a week is conducive to reaching those results.

We give you our best wishes and hope you enjoy this workout and are soon realising the benefits as you naturally progress through the different levels, happily improving the quality of your life.

Stay fit, healthy and happy. Enjoy life!

Dina and Mark

Glossary

Back muscles

A group of muscles located from the skull, down the spine, to the hip, attaching to the collarbone, shoulder blade and above the upper arm. They are responsible for depression (lowering), adduction (closer to the body) of the shoulder blades, extension (bringing back) and adduction of the upper arm at the shoulder joint.

Bicep

A muscle located at the shoulder blade and shoulder joint, going through the shoulder and elbow and attaching to the top of the forearm. It is responsible for flexion (bringing forward) of the upper arm at the shoulder joint, and flexion (bending) at the elbow.

Chest muscles

A group of muscles located at the sternum, collarbone and ribs that attach to the top of the upper arm and shoulder blades. They are responsible for horizontal flexion, flexion, adduction (closer to the body), internal rotation of the upper arm at the shoulder joint and depression (lowering), abduction (away from the body) and protraction (bringing forward) of the shoulder blades.

Drawing the Core Muscles In & Up - Navel/Spine

The feeling of pulling the navel deep down internally and anchoring the back down to the floor as if there is a great weight pressing down, and drawing the tummy up underneath the rib cage.

Gluteus Maximus and Medius

The group of muscles located at the pelvis attaching to the top of the thigh bone, responsible for extension (straightening), and the inward and outward turning of the upper leg at the hip joint.

Hamstrings

The group of muscles located at the pelvis that run down the hip, the back of the thigh and knee attaching to the lower leg. They are responsible for flexion (straightening) at the hip and flexing the leg, bending at the knee joint.

Hip flexors

Two muscles located at the hip, responsible for flexion (raising the upper leg) at the hip joint.

Lengthening

Conceptualising the body being pulled upward from the crown of the head, reaching out and extending from the spine.

Obliques (External and Internal)

Side abdominal muscles located at the ribs and hip, responsible for flexion, side flexion and rotation in the torso.

Quadriceps

The group of muscles located at the hip running down the front of the thigh and attaching to the knee cap and above the shin. They are responsible for extending the leg, straightening at the knee joint.

Rectus Abdominus

The superficial abdominal muscles in the pelvis that attach to the ribs and sternum, responsible for flexion, side flexion and rotation of the trunk or spine.

Transverse Abdominus

Deep abdominal muscles located at the hip and lower spine, attaching to the abdominal wall responsible for reducing the circumference of the abdomen, bracing the lower spine and drawing the abdominal region inward toward the spine.

Triceps

The group of muscles located at the shoulder blade and upper arm, running down the back of the shoulder, arms and through the elbow, attaching to the forearm. They are responsible for extension (bringing backward) of the upper arm at the shoulder and extension (straightening) of the arm at the elbow joint.

ABOUT THE AUTHORS

DINA MATTY

DINA is a trained dancer, aerobics champion and expert fitness teacher. Her study of dance in England led her to an exciting professional career that saw her on television and videos around the world. Dina then took up aerobics and became the UK and European champion over two years. She has since studied pilates and is passionate about the art and the benefits. Her studies under master teachers Romana Kryzanowska and Cynthia Lochard at the New York Pilates Studio in Sydney have made her dedicated to teaching Joseph H. Pilates' original format, and she is intent on furthering her studies to become a teacher trainer. Dina is now settled in Australia on the Gold Coast in Queensland where she is the proprietor of Pulse Health Studio in Niecon Tower in Broadbeach.

MARK RICHARDSON

MARK discovered martial arts in Japan at the age of six and became a student of Kyokushinkai Karate on the Gold Coast in Queensland at ten. His love of the art and his competition experience sparked an interest in boxing and other martial arts, developing a positive attitude and interest in health and fitness. Mark studied sports management and marketing at Griffith University and exercise science at the AIF. His studies have led him towards a career as a personal trainer alongside Dina at Pulse Health Studio in Niecon Tower in Broadbeach and as a karate instructor.

BOTH DINA AND MARK'S experience has previously given Dina the opportunity to present the DVD and book *Pilates the Authentic Way*, and Mark to present *Fighting Fit*. Now Dina and Mark are pleased to bring you their fitball and resistance band workout book and DVD *Simply Ball & Band*, and know that it will offer you a range of challenges whilst keeping the training fun. Look out for Dina and Mark in future releases in pilates, martial arts, and cardio and strength training, so that you can add to the variety of your overall health, fitness and well being.